THE
COUNTRY CLUB

BY
DOUGLAS CARTER BEANE

★

★

DRAMATISTS
PLAY SERVICE
INC.

"The Country Club" was first produced by
The Dorset Theatre Festival
Directed by
Edgar Lansbury

World Premiere Production
Presented at
Long Wharf Theatre

Doug Hughes	Michael Ross
Artistic Director	Managing Director

Original New York Production
Produced by Drama Dept.
www.dramadept.com

for Cynthia Nixon

Everything happens at parties.

—Jane Austen

THE COUNTRY CLUB was produced by Drama Dept. (Douglas Carter Beane, Artistic Director; Michael S. Rosenberg, Managing Director) at the Greenwich House Theater in New York City on September 29, 1999. It was directed by Christopher Ashley; the set design was by James M. Youmans; the lighting design was by Frances Aronsen; the sound design was by Laura Grace Brown; the costume design was by Jonathan Bixby; and the stage manager was John Handy. The cast was as follows:

POOKER	Amy Hohn
SOOS	Cynthia Nixon
FROGGY	Amy Sedaris
BRI	Peter Benson
ZIP	Tom Everett Scott
HUTCH	Fredrick Weller
CHLOE	Callie Thorne

During the run, the cast was joined by T. Scott Cunningham, Jessica Stone, Albert Macklin, Ross Gibby and Savanne Martin.

THE COUNTRY CLUB premiered at the Dorset Theater Festival and had a production in Los Angeles by the SEJ Group. It had its regional theater debut at the Long Wharf Theater under the watchful and encouraging eye of Doug Hughes (who helped this play in many large ways).

CAST OF CHARACTERS

SOOS — For Susan. A handsome woman. Like the rest of the cast, in the latter half of her twenties or early thirties. Her clothing and manner are a little more sophisticated than the others.

POOKER — Her real name is Patricia. Pretty, in an eccentric way. Slightly kooky, extremely droll.

FROGGY — Spunk. And all that confidence that goes with shopping almost exclusively from Brooks Brothers. A bundle of nervous energy ready to snap at any moment.

BRI — For Brian. Married to Froggy and not originally from Wyomissing. Bespectacled and well-groomed. Despite being so well assembled, he always seems a little uncomfortable.

ZIP — His real name is Thomas Mueller. With his classic good looks, solid build, year-round tan, intelligence, charm and business sense, he is a hope for tomorrow. Unfortunately, in his late twenties (or early thirties) and still working for his father, the hope seems a little forced.

HUTCH — For Gregg Hutchenson. Zip's best friend. But then, just about everybody's best friend. His hair is always unkempt, his clothing always a little disheveled.

CHLOE — Full name: Chloe Maria Donna DeGlatalia. Beautiful. Her Mediterranean looks are a direct contrast to the Anglo-Saxons. So is her matter-of-fact directness. A slight South Philadelphia dialect.

SETTING

Outside the small industrial town of Reading, Pennsylvania, is an affluent suburb called Wyomissing. On the outskirts of the suburb is a country club with tennis courts and a golf course. The play takes place in the enclosed porch of the Wyomissing Country Club. Decorations change with each holiday celebration. The time is the present year.

THE COUNTRY CLUB

ACT ONE

Scene 1

"Happy New Year"

From the ballroom we hear the music and laughter of a party. The French doors swing open; Pooker and Soos enter.

SOOS.   Talk talk talk. All this talk and no one is saying anything. Do you have a light?

POOKER.   I quit.

SOOS.   Turncoat! Pook, you seriously must teach me. I know I grew up here, but I've been away and forgotten. How do you speak Wyomissing, Pennsylvania? There must be matches in here somewhere. How do you say something without saying it?

POOKER.   Easy as complete and total pie. You'll pick it up in no time. Give me an example and I'll translate it into country club.

SOOS.   Oh. OK. Uhm. How do you say someone is Jewish?

POOKER.   Jewish? "What a character!"

SOOS.   I need matches.

POOKER.   Why?

SOOS.   I'm going to burn myself down.

POOKER.   You asked, I told.

SOOS.   I'm sorry but for the last couple of years my consciousness has been raised.

POOKER.   You too? Isn't it the worst?

SOOS.   Forget it. So, how do I say someone's black in country-club speak?

POOKER. "So well-spoken."

SOOS. Sadly, that I remember.

POOKER. It's like Latin it comes back to you.

SOOS. This is the cub room, for the kids to hang and smoke, where's the big ol' bowl o' matches?

POOKER. Try the mug on the coffee table.

SOOS. Having a miracle. *(She pulls out matches and reads them.)* "Muffin and Trip, Happy Wedding Day."

POOKER. Who are Muffin and Trip?

SOOS. I don't know, but I love them. *(She strikes. Nothing.)* These matches are soggy.

POOKER. Give me a hard one. I'll translate from English to WASP. Go.

SOOS. Uhm. "I know your husband is a premature ejaculator because he entirely pounced me in the cloakroom and ruined my best Caroline Herrera."

POOKER. *(Thinks a moment, then.)* "Please pass the peas."

SOOS. All this circuity, thank God, I'm only here for two weeks. I mean how would I say, "I moved to California for my husband, and then he left me"?

POOKER. I think you just did. Soos. Did you and Walker have a split?

SOOS. As you would say, "complete and total." Where are there matches?

POOKER. I'm sorry to hear that.

SOOS. Big beautiful nightmare. Had something like a nervous breakdown. Seriously had to go somewhere and like "rest." Let's not talk about it.

POOKER. *(Lifting an old wooden lighter.)* Here we are.

SOOS. Ta da. *(Taking the lighter.)*

POOKER. Shame. I kind of liked Walker. He seemed OK.

SOOS. Oh. He was. More than OK even. He was. Passionate and fiery and strong. And gentle and … really kind of sincere. And he listened to me. Truly listened. But then he went and stopped loving me. Didn't count on that.

POOKER. Like sex like?

SOOS. No, more breakfast. It was this one breakfast. And I was talking about, actually more jagging I'm sure, if I know me the way I know me, about the pool man. And I looked across the table and I noticed he wasn't with me. He was looking at me, but behind his eyes, it looked like, I don't know, Muzak was playing in his head or something. I changed the subject and looked away but still. Behind those eyes. He was hearing the theme to "A Summer Place." Or "The Girl from Ipanema." Or. And I knew on this stupid spinning planet there was only one person I truly cared about. And I was numbing him. About two months later he moved out. I wonder what song was playing in his head when I asked him to stay.

POOKER.   Oh Susan.

SOOS.   Poor Susan. Boo hoo. Let's have a pity party for Soos. *(She tries the lighter. It is dead. She looks heavenward.)*

POOKER.   Are you hoping to see Zip while you're in town? Still have a complete and total crush on him?

SOOS.   Thomas Benum Mueller the Third? A.k.a. "Zip" Mueller? Oh, Please. How is he?

POOKER.   He still looks at every woman like she would be so lucky to have him. The man is selling real estate in Pennsylvania, you think that would humble a person.

SOOS.   Where is he tonight?

POOKER.   With Hutch running naked in the woods.

SOOS.   This is so good I'm going to stop looking for matches. What?

POOKER.   Zip and Hutch, thrashing off the creeping ennui two New Year's Eves ago, decided to take off all their clothing, take BB guns and shoot at the complete and total racist lawn jockey on Old Lady Gertz's driveway. They've been doing it ever since.

SOOS.   Why?

POOKER.   I don't know, they were bored.

SOOS.   So boredom is now an excuse for deranged behavior?

POOKER.   Fully. Anyway Zip doesn't have a girlfriend. Hutch is engaged, do you believe it? Some girl from Philly. I have a boyfriend.

SOOS.   What more could you possibly want?

POOKER.   A cute boyfriend.

FROGGY.   *(Offstage.)* Someone's in the cub room, see, Brian, someone's in the cub room. Let's go in the cub room.

SOOS. Oh my God, people actually still call it the cub room. *(The French doors swing open to reveal Froggy and her husband Bri. There is much ad-libbed squealing and hugging. Everyone then stops and sighs; there is a moment of silence. Then —)* Do either of you have a light?

FROGGY. Am I overwhelmed, I am OVERwhelmed, Patricia and Susan, old home week, you know my husband, Brian.

SOOS. No. Susan Walker. It's a pleasure to meet you.

FROGGY. Brian and I have been married for six months — it's a shame you couldn't come but you were off in California having fun, but it was a very elegant affair. It was probably the most sophisticated thing these hicks around here have ever seen. We had it in the ballroom, which was all done with calla lilies sent in from Amsterdam. And it was a sit-down which we had catered, not the club chef who is, *entre nous,* very lousy. And we had them use the chandelier with the real candles and Wes Carpenter played music from his classical folder and … *(Dramatically, she points to herself.)* The gown.

SOOS. The gown?

FROGGY. The gown.

SOOS. *(Looking to Pooker for help.)* The gown?

POOKER. *(With a mocking brightness.)* The gown.

FROGGY. Just, the gown. I tell you the whole thing was quite, quite elegant, everything was white and silver and the bridesmaids! Guess what color the bridesmaids wore, guess, you'll never guess.

SOOS. White and silver?

FROGGY. *(Laughing at the thought.)* No. Guess again.

SOOS. I don't know, peach?

FROGGY. Black.

SOOS. *(Unable to hide her shock.)* Black? Wasn't that a little … funereal?

POOKER. Wait.

FROGGY. You'd think it would be, but they were all sewn up with sequins, very chic, and the guests — the men wore tuxedos, they had to, it said so right on the invitation. And the women could wear whatever they wanted as long as they had — *(She points to Bri.)*

BRI. *(Barely audible.)* Sequins.

FROGGY. Right, Brian, sequins on them and it was so elegant that the Reverend Bertner, we married Episcopalian (it's for the best), anyway the Reverend Bertner was so stunned by the beauty he looked up at the room in the middle of the service and said, "Holy Christ, it looks like an old episode of *Dynasty*." He was so stunned. By the beauty.

BRI. He was also Episcopalian and had a lot of sherry in him.

FROGGY. Nobody cares about doing weddings correctly anymore. They just throw them together. We went to Muffin and Trip's wedding last weekend —

BRI. Tacky, very tacky.

FROGGY. It was very tacky.

SOOS. Their matches sucked.

FROGGY. People are forgetful of the fact that weddings are events and events are important because they make the rest of the days so bearable. I know I could wake up in the morning with this, you know cold feeling of terror and then, I'll remember I have a birthday party, or a Halloween party, and I'll cheer right up. A Christmas party, a wedding —

POOKER. A *bris*.

FROGGY. A what?

SOOS. It's a Jewish thing.

FROGGY. Jewish? What a character! How's your marriage, Susan?

SOOS. Well, it's over.

FROGGY. Ooops. Sorry. Faux pas. Open mouth, insert foot.

SOOS. You don't have a light on you by any chance?

FROGGY. We don't smoke. We must get together. Seems like old times. Patricia and Susan.

SOOS. C'mon. Don't be so formal. This is Pooker and Soos.

FROGGY. I don't like nicknames.

SOOS. Oh, Froggy, why don't you like nicknames?

FROGGY. Louise. My name is Louise.

SOOS. Sorry. *(An awkward pause.)*

FROGGY. Well Brian and I are going to dance. Wes Carpenter is playing our song, come join us.

SOOS. Gee. No. Bad luck. Three on a man.

POOKER.   That's three on a match.

SOOS.   Don't say "match."

POOKER.   Sorry.

SOOS.   But go dance and come back soon. You'll know where to find us. The cub room.

FROGGY.   It really is super having you back. *(Bri escorts Froggy out. Soos walks over and slams the door behind them.)*

SOOS.   That's why I'm afraid to stay more than two weeks. By the third week, they would make sense.

POOKER.   Uh, such the rage? And you only saw Froggy. I can only imagine what you'll do when you see Cookie Dibble.

SOOS.   Oh jeez. I'm upset, aren't I? It's just that I've worked so hard to ignore the influence of these people and to suddenly see them alive and well and in lifelike 3-D, it's just — I shouldn't get upset. I've been upset way too much lately. I mean if I actually pause to consider how Froggy — excuse me, Louise — is behaving, I will probably just take something big and pointed and jab her. I mean, do you remember Froggy? How just seriously aware she was? Do you remember how, during an assembly on the importance of picking the right college, she stood up on her chair? And just started singing? At the top of her lungs? "Love IS a Battlefield"? She was always centered and knowing and sarcastic as fuck and. Not Louise-like. At all. I. I need. I need a light, is what I need.

POOKER.   Soos, it'll be midnight soon. Let's hit the ballroom for the countdown.

SOOS.   No, that's too — that would be too much.

POOKER.   There are sure to be matches there.

SOOS.   No, I like it here.

POOKER.   Lighters. Bic Lighters.

SOOS.   No, I'll — I like it here.

POOKER.   Well I am but completely and totally prepared to wish in the New Year in the ballroom.

SOOS.   Go. Don't worry about it. Just bring me back some matches.

POOKER.   Please come.

SOOS.   No really. The thought of Wes Carpenter's rendition of "Auld Lang Syne" is enough to destroy a whole new year for me.

POOKER.   OK. If you say so. Be back in a bit. *(Pooker exits, leaving the door open behind her. Soos stands still for a moment soaking in the sound of the party. Without warning, the countdown begins, at "10." Soos is startled out of her trance. She walks over to the door and slams it. She locks the door and turns off the overhead light. Grabbing a pillow, she curls up on a sofa. The party begins to sing "Auld Lang Syne." Soos is crying as she gently rocks back and forth. Suddenly there is a rap on the window. Scared, Soos runs to a corner to hide. The window swings open and Zip, naked, stumbles in. He is quite drunk and laughing hysterically. He makes his way to a section of the room where his clothing is hidden. Hutch, also naked, appears at the window, trying to say something, but laughing too hard. Soos wipes away her tears, smiles, walks to the center of the room and displays her cigarette. Trying to make out the shadowy figure, Zip goes to her.)*

ZIP.   Soos?

SOOS.   Hello, Zip. You wouldn't happen to have a light on you, would you?

Scene 2

"Martin Luther King Day"

The New Year's Eve decorations are gone, replaced with "Happy Martin Luther King Day" signs and symbols. A dance is going on in the ballroom. Pooker sits on the back of a sofa drinking a beer. Froggy sits on the floor in front of Bri who, while reading a magazine, is massaging her neck with his free hand.

FROGGY.   *WELL* Soos said she was going to be here two weeks and we are looking at week three here, (are we not?), I mean she said she was coming back home to screw her head back on (could she be more California, I ask you? — cuckoo cuckoo). Soos and

Zip? Back together. Better believe it. — Both hands Brian, more strength — Zip needs her. All great men need greater women behind them. Look at Brian. That's why lesbians seem to do so well for themselves. Two women. Speaking of which you might not want to sit that way, Pooker. Now, I love Zip, despite what you may hear, but he has been just so unbearable since he got out of college, I mean he just decides after four years of college that he doesn't want to work in his major? *(Mockingly.)* "Oh Louise, I can't go into politics, I don't believe in anything." *(Normal voice.)* I told him, I said, "Zip, get elected and you'll find something to believe in." It was about this time that he started throwing things at me. — Brian, lower! *(Pause.)* Salted peanuts, napkins, bottle tops, swizzle sticks — Brian, do it like a man. Make pretend. — Zip and Soos are back TO-GE-THER and everything is returning to its perfect cosmic place. — Brian, what are you possibly reading?

POOKER. The marriage certificate for loopholes.

BRI. Some club membership brochure magazine jobbie.

FROGGY. Why?

BRI. I just want to see how they tactfully say something.

POOKER. What?

BRI. No blacks and no Jews.

POOKER. It's in the first sentence. "Enjoy our country club atmosphere."

FROGGY. Before we move on to talking about whatever Brian is reading —

HUTCH. *(Entering.)* Hey.

BRI. Hi Hutch, how are you?

HUTCH. I am so wasted.

FROGGY. That's who you really should marry.

POOKER. Who?

FROGGY. Hutch.

HUTCH. What?

POOKER. Frogs, what is this complete and total match-up thing you are doing here? Has God spoken to you? Are you building an ark? Hutch and I are already mated. Hutch has a fiancée in Philly and I have a boyfriend who isn't cute whom I love.

FROGGY. Oh.

POOKER. So —

SOOS. *(Entering with Zip.)* Zipper, Happy Martin Luther King Day —

ZIP. The Junior League has a dream.

SOOS. I'm surprised to see Cookie Dibble here.

ZIP. Really, she's so much more of a Malcolm X person.

FROGGY. Zip and Soos together talking and me having no idea what they are talking about. It's just like old times.

POOKER. Frog one, cease and desist.

SOOS. What's she on about?

POOKER. Froggy is organizing everyone's life for them.

FROGGY. I'm sorry, but when your formative years are the Reagan/Bush years, it's hard not to think of the present day as something of a comedown. *Disillusion* is my watchword.

ZIP. Disillusion. As in moving away from or the negative of ... illusion? And this somehow is a bad thing? *(All except Froggy and Bri laugh.)*

FROGGY. Mocking, mocking, everybody mocking. I just want everyone to be happy.

SOOS. And would Zip and I be happier if we were together?

FROGGY. I smell Sterno, has the buffet started?

SOOS. Just now.

ZIP. Old Lady Gertz is staring incredulously at a plate of chitlins.

FROGGY. Brian wants something to eat. *(Bri looks up. He does?)* You know, Zip —

ZIP. You want something, Soos?

FROGGY. You know, Zip —

SOOS. Nothing, I'm so fat.

ZIP. Yeah right.

HUTCH. You going to the buffet, Zipper?

FROGGY. You know, Zip, I was talking to my daddy about the whole you-going-into-politics-thing and he said — *(Zip casually reaches over to the end table, picks up a magazine and throws it at Froggy.)* ZIP!! Bri, Zip just threw a *Town and Country* at me.

ZIP. What's on the buffet?

HUTCH. Chicken and ribs I think.

FROGGY. Bri, say something.

BRI. Zip, don't throw magazines at Froggy.

FROGGY. Louise! *(Pooker, Hutch, Froggy and Bri exit into the ballroom. Zip and Soos laugh at Froggy.)*

SOOS. Is it me or does Froggy have Bri —

ZIP. Man, what's with him?

SOOS. Right by the —

ZIP. He puts up with it.

SOOS. I mean, Carpe Scrotum. *(They laugh.)*

ZIP. He is no longer male. We are revoking his license.

SOOS. I'd stop speaking to him, but we are going to their house for drinks.

ZIP. So is Froggy now thinking that we're getting back together.

SOOS. Utterly. She's mad. So mad.

ZIP. They probably all are.

SOOS. Mad?

ZIP. Well. Thinking we're getting back together.

SOOS. Probably.

ZIP. You think?

SOOS. Oh. Of course. You know they're just expecting you to take me back to your place in Flying Hills and just — it's breathtaking in its stupidity.

ZIP. Well, I mean I can't blame them thinking it. We did date for a long time.

SOOS. There's that. And we get along. But I mean. The idea is —

ZIP. Horrific.

SOOS. There's that.

ZIP. And we know each other *SO* well.

SOOS. There's definitely that. No mystery.

ZIP. That. *So* that. It would be — I mean if we were together, we would have to giggle. *(They laugh.)* And sport matching attire —

SOOS. It's too impossible.

ZIP. And have potentially really kind of good sex. *(This surprises them both. The laughter fades. A pause. Soos thinks for a moment. Has a sip of her drink, then thinks for a moment more.)*

SOOS. There's that. *(They look at one another and smile.)*

ZIP. There is that.

SOOS. Would you want to?

ZIP.   Would you?

SOOS.   So, after Froggy's tonight? Flying Hills?

ZIP.   I'm thinking more in terms of the whole Flying Hills thing now.

SOOS.   I can live with that. *(They slowly exit.)* We'll just have to come up with a decent excuse for not going to Froggy's.

ZIP.   How about, "You're shrill"? *(They are offstage.)*

Scene 3

"Valentine's Day"

The lights are on; the door is open. Chloe walks in. Her appearance is a direct contrast to the other women in the club. Her clothing is red and revealing. She sashays over to the window and looks out. Without breaking concentration, she effortlessly finds her cigarette and lights it. She takes a long, luxurious drag. Zip walks in. He goes over to the sofa and picks up Soos' purse. He looks at Chloe. She looks back. She looks away.

ZIP.   Hello.

CHLOE.   Hello. *(Pause.)*

ZIP.   Hello hello.

CHLOE.   Hello. *(Pause.)*

ZIP.   Great night.

CHLOE.   Yeah. *(Pause.)*

ZIP.   Happy, uhm Valentine's day.

CHLOE.   Thanks. Same to you.

ZIP.   It's nice out here, isn't it?

CHLOE.   Yeah. Very relaxing.

ZIP.   You're not a member.

CHLOE.   No. I'm a guest. They had a name tag for me to wear. It said, "Hello, my name is Chloe. I'm a guest." I told my date that if I wore a sign that said, "Hello, my name is Chloe. I'm a guest," the evening would end with a body count. He said I didn't have to wear it.

ZIP.   That was very nice of him.

CHLOE.   Yeah. I thought so.

ZIP.   So.

CHLOE.   Yeah?

ZIP.   Your name is Chloe.

CHLOE.   Very good.

ZIP.   And you're a guest. You're somebody's date? No — don't tell me. Farmer's?

CHLOE.   No, I —

ZIP.   Sketchy's? No. You are someone's date?

CHLOE.   This is a Valentine's Day dance. I didn't show up stag.

ZIP.   Yes. Are you dating this guy?

CHLOE.   I don't think you can call it dating. You see, we're —

ZIP.   That's good to hear. Because I might want to ask you out.

CHLOE.   No, wait. Are you being charming? Is this charming?

ZIP.   Yes. Sure. *(Pause.)*

CHLOE.   My. You're charming the pants right offa me. I gotta go.

ZIP.   I'm sorry, am I upsetting you?

CHLOE.   I'm teasing. I got to get back.

ZIP.   So, are you from the greater Reading area?

CHLOE.   Uh, no. Philadelphia. And you're from Wyomissing?

ZIP.   Yeah. And I'm not dating anyone.

CHLOE.   You're not? And that's yours? The purse?

ZIP.   Yes.

CHLOE.   It goes like a dream with the suit.

ZIP.   It's not mine. It's my date's.

CHLOE.   But you're not dating.

ZIP.   It's nothing. Your eyes are like deep or something.

CHLOE.   I heard. Tell me more about this not-really date.

ZIP.   It's nothing. Just someone to go to the club with. An old friend. A — you know.

CHLOE.   I'm sorry. I don't. I'm not a club sort of person.

ZIP.   Just an old friend that acts like a date. For social events. Not someone I love or anything.

CHLOE.   Does she know this? This club date?

ZIP. Yes. Of course. God, yes. I think. Well, you know. I mean it's not something we discuss at great lengths. Well, you know, you're with someone you're not dating anymore. So I mean —

CHLOE. That's not what I was —

ZIP. First of all, dating? That's language archeology there, right? I'm sorry, you were saying?

CHLOE. I —

ZIP. God, I do that, don't I? I just jump in when I want to hear what some lady I'm attracted to is saying. I hope that doesn't bother you.

CHLOE. It doesn't bother me. I don't think you under — I'd better be gettin' back. It was nice talkin' to you.

ZIP. Nice view.

CHLOE. What?

ZIP. The golf course.

CHLOE. Right.

ZIP. You wanna kiss?

CHLOE. *(Startled.)* What?

ZIP. Please?

CHLOE. No.

ZIP. Why not?

CHLOE. I don't know you well enough to kiss you.

ZIP. Oh.

CHLOE. I've got to go.

ZIP. Stay. Do you want me to change the subject?

CHLOE. I'm leaving.

ZIP. Are you sure you don't want to kiss me?

CHLOE. No. That's why I want to leave. *(He kisses her.)* What are you doin'? God, don't do that. *(A pause. She thinks about what has happened. She slaps him.)* Ouch. Sorry. Now ... stop that. OK? I don't know you well enough. And besides, I —

ZIP. What would you like to know?

CHLOE. Nothing. Anything. Please leave. Nothing. Your name.

ZIP. My friends call me Zip.

CHLOE. Why?

ZIP. I don't know, that's my nickname. Can I kiss you again?

CHLOE. No. I'm going.

ZIP. Stay.

CHLOE. How come that's your nickname?

ZIP. I don't — it was my uncle's nickname. I have no idea. Can I kiss you again?

CHLOE. No. God. You're drunk.

ZIP. I am not.

CHLOE. Get outta here!

ZIP. It was a good kiss

CHLOE. It was a very nice kiss, but that's not the point. The point is that you're drunk and you don't know what your nickname means and you assaulted me just now and this is the second rudest club I've ever been in. If they have a wet T-shirt contest it'll be tied for first. What am I talking about?

ZIP. Where are you going?

CHLOE. We'll just pretend this whole little whatever-it-was never happened. OK?

ZIP. OK. Do you want to kiss again?

CHLOE. Are you brain-damaged? *(With an attempt at sign language.)* I'm leaving.

ZIP. No, let me go. I'll go. I'm sorry. You stay. Me leave. *(He leaves, but stops at the door.)* Hey, Chloe! *(She turns around.)* You're a lovely guest. *(He is gone.)*

CHLOE. *(A moment. She takes a long drag of her cigarette and looks out the window.)* What an asshole. *(The lights fade as she puts her cigarette out.)*

Scene 4

"St. Patrick's Day"

In a tribute to Ireland, Hutch and Zip are wearing green sweaters and are drunk. Hutch is standing on the sofa; Zip is sitting on the floor pounding a drum improvised from an overturned wastepaper basket.

HUTCH. This is Gregg Hutchenson.

ZIP. *(Pounding on the drum.)* Das right.

HUTCH. And this be Thomas Mueller.

ZIP. *(Pounding on the drum.)* Right on right on.

HUTCH. We is Hutch and Zip. *(Zip pounds the drum.)* And we dance just as good as we want. *(They go nuts. Hutch singing the "Tighten' up" riff and dancing, Zip pounding his drum and ad-libbing cries of "Rock on with your bad self." They eventually explode into laughter and catch their breath.*

ZIP. Rock on with your bad self.

HUTCH. That was the fun.

ZIP. The fun.

HUTCH. The *only* fun. Breakin' into my dad's 45 collection and dancin'.

ZIP. White people dancin' to black music. The very best fun. Then your dad would show up —

HUTCH. Fucking Roger. He would just waddle down 'round midnight all full of brew and — you remember this? — we'd be like dancing and he'd be lit and he'd take a sponge, clean off the bar and just keep saying over and over again, "Boys, always keep a clean bar." *(Pause.)* "It doesn't matter if you're rich, it doesn't matter if you're poor. Always keep a clean bar."

ZIP. I remember that.

HUTCH. Then he'd pass out. I fucking hate him.

ZIP. Roger? Nah. He's a good guy.

HUTCH. I don't hate him. Just the getting drunk. Repeating himself. Passing out. I will never be like that.

ZIP. It was fun, he'd pass out we could pinch some beer.

HUTCH. Fuck that was fun. Fucking Roger would just waddle down 'round midnight all full of brew and —

ZIP. You just said that.

HUTCH. You sure?

ZIP. I was here, I heard you.

HUTCH. Fuck me.

ZIP. That was fun, though.

HUTCH. We were like … close then.

ZIP. *(Pause.)* Yeah. Guess we were. That was before there were women. Before we were —

HUTCH. In competition. How many women were we in competition for do you think?

ZIP. Hundre —

HUTCH. Thous —

ZIP. Millio —

HUTCH. Bazillio —

ZIP. Every woman known to man, I guess.

HUTCH. Ha!! Can't happen now. No way, Jose. 'Cause I be gettin' married and shit.

ZIP. No way, Jose.

HUTCH. Hey, when are you gonna get married?

ZIP. Me? Oh God I — women are pretty much a quagmire for me.

HUTCH. A quagmire.

ZIP. Yeah. Quagmire. I mean, I don't need them, then one of 'em fucking invades my life. Sex becomes an obsession. Then when I get to know them it's not the sex I'm after, it's the company. So I go and orchestrate all these goofy-ass chance encounters. "Oh, hello." But I'm afraid she'll reject me or whatever so I take my time. Then someone else comes along and — or has already come along and — I always sing the right note. But the song is over.

HUTCH. Quagmire.

ZIP. Right.

HUTCH. Nice use of a vocab word in a sentence. Hey, when you gettin' married?

24

ZIP. You just —

HUTCH. Fuck me. OK. New topic. Do you love her?

ZIP. Uh, who?

HUTCH. Chloe. My fiancée. Doof. Do you love her?

ZIP. Oh, yeah. Chloe? She's the best. Nice lady.

HUTCH. Bullshit. Bullshit on rye. You want her so bad. It's so friggin' obvious. And guess what? I got her. After all that, Hutch got the beauty. You are the loser for once. Life is good. I'll get the beer, the victor buys! And that is a whole new topic. HA!

ZIP. Actually, you said that about an hour ago.

HUTCH. Oh. Fuck me.

ZIP. *(Sadly.)* Fuck me.

Scene 5

"April Fools'"

The lights come up on the April Fools' Day decorated cub room. Soos and Zip are in the middle of an argument.

SOOS. *(Quickly.)* Don't say another word. Just cannot handle another word. I'm just like — why do you have to choose a party to tell me — I'm like confused enough already. I don't even know what I'm celebrating anymore. I just keep coming to these parties. It's like this bell goes off and I stagger back to where I was before like a punch-drunk fighter. I mean, what is this? April Fools'? I mean, shit.

ZIP. Soos —

SOOS. Any excuse to have a party. And this has to be the lamest of holidays. April Fools' Day? I am so sure. I wake up this morning. My mother informs me that she needs my room to convert back into a sewing room. I inform her that she still has Chipper's room and Cuffy's room and has had them for quite some time. She tells me that she has some big women's auxiliary

THANG and needs all three rooms and I'm furious. Well, just as I'm about to launch, she jumps up and shouts, "April Fools!" And I'm like, "Gee, Mom, today at the hospital are you going to tell crippled people that they can walk?" I mean let's be brutal, why don't we? What is the purpose of this day? Practical jokes? Humiliation? They should call this Humiliation Day and let it go at that. And then the bank —

ZIP.   Soos. We have to talk.

SOOS.   No we don't.

ZIP.   We do.

SOOS.   Of course we do. I know we do. And I know what you're going to say. What you started to say. I saw it in your eyes. It was in your eyes when you picked me up this evening. I'm a woman, I know that look. All women know that look. Mothers train their daughters for that look. There are flash cards with that look on them.

ZIP.   You know what I'm going to say?

SOOS.   Why do you think I've been babbling like a Nazi spy on truth serum? I don't want to hear you say it. You aren't going to say it, right?

ZIP.   C'mon, Soos. You deserve better.

SOOS.   There's a new angle. *(Pause.)*

ZIP.   You deserve to be loved. To be in love. To have someone in love with you. *(Pause.)* You know I care for you.

SOOS.   Of course. Of course.

ZIP.   I mean we've known each other since like forever.

SOOS.   Before that even.

ZIP.   And we're very comfortable together. Like an old friend.

SOOS.   Like an old friend.

ZIP.   But — that's not what a love affair should be. There should be like passion and joy and junk like that. Feelings.

SOOS.   Right.

ZIP.   I want more. Don't you?

SOOS.   I had more. I don't want more again. I want this.

ZIP.   I think you deserve better.

SOOS.   You love that angle. Yes. Well. Maybe I should be the judge of what I deserve. *(Pause.)* So, it's over?

ZIP.   *(Pause.)* Yes. I'm sorry. *(Pause. Then with significance.)* I'm

26

sorry.

SOOS.   It's OK. It still hurts. But, it's OK.

ZIP.   OK.

SOOS.   Is there someone else?

ZIP.   Yes.

SOOS.   Ahhhh.

ZIP.   But she's with someone else. Someone I respect, so it wouldn't be … classy. She doesn't even know. It's a from-afar kind of thing.

SOOS.   What are you going to do?

ZIP.   I don't know. What can I do? Nothing, I guess. I don't know. What are you going to do?

SOOS.   I — well, I think it's time for me to move on. To California, maybe. Or New York. Or Paris. Paris would be cool. I'd like to live somewhere where everyone spoke a condescending language and was rude to me. I think it would be like living in a restaurant. I'd like that.

ZIP.   You're crazy, I lo — I'm very fond of you. *(Pause.)* Still friends? *(He puts his hand out. Long pause.)*

SOOS.   I guess there's no chance of you suddenly yelling, "April Fools." *(She looks at his hand.)* I didn't think so. *(They shake hands.)*

ZIP.   When are you going to leave?

SOOS.   Should I look for a ride?

ZIP.   No, not from the club. From Wyo.

SOOS.   I don't know. I don't know if I'm ready. I don't know if I'm going to leave. Yet. *(Pause.)* When I was in Bible school they told us that girls would be seduced by worldly things. Like diamonds and fame and emeralds and men that look like Parker Stevenson. But we're not. We're seduced by status quo. *(Pause.)* I'll probably be gone after this weekend.

ZIP.   Right. Sorry.

SOOS.   Don't say "sorry."

ZIP.   Right. You all right?

SOOS.   Of course.

ZIP.   I'll see you.

SOOS.   Of course. *(He exits. Soos is alone.)* Of course. *(The lights fade.)*

Scene 6

"A June Wedding"

The band swings through a bright tarantella. The lights come up on the cub room, which is decorated for Chloe and Hutch's wedding. Froggy, Pooker and Bri are present and seated. Uncomfortably. Not quite knowing what to say. There is a long pause, then ...

BRI.   Well. Now. Golly. It certainly was nice of the DeGlatalias' to throw a wedding for Chloe and Hutch. *(There are shouts offstage. Their composure falls.)* Oh my God.
FROGGY.   Oh, Hutch.
POOKER.   Oh, Hutch, Hutch, Hutch.
BRI.   Poor Hutch.
FROGGY.   What have you gotten yourself into?
POOKER.   I weep for Hutch. I truly do. Chloe is like —
FROGGY.   The whole family is like —
BRI.   Fatal error.
POOKER.   A complete and total —
BRI.   Fatal error. The dress?
POOKER.   Cheap, cheap, cheap.
FROGGY.   She looks like Susan Lucci. Why would anyone want to look like Susan Lucci?
BRI.   And the men's suits?
POOKER.   Krass Brother's South Street. Store of the Stars.
FROGGY.   And the service? With the gum chewing?
POOKER.   I am like, "Hutch, love is like blind or like what?"
BRI.   And relatives? As entertainment?
POOKER.   And making those like so embarrassing toasts in Italian. And crying and just saying it all in Italian and —
FROGGY.   Did they think we understood Italian?
POOKER.   The only word I understand is "bella." Whenever

28

they say "bella" in a speech I just kind of shout out. I think it fits in.

FROGGY.   What is Hutch going to do with this family? I can only imagine.

BRI.   He really could have done better.

POOKER.   And the woman with the bazooms?

BRI.   The aunt. Scary.

POOKER.   You could place things on her breasts.

BRI.   Very scary.

POOKER.   She's like this walking breakfront.

FROGGY.   OK, I'm going to out-and-out say it. I've suppressed my true feelings long enough. I'm going to say it. Out-and-out. Chloe DeGlatalia … is … a climber. She's climbing. There. I've said it. Out-and-out. Need I say more? End of discussion. *(She sits down.)* I rest my case.

ZIP.   *(Enters.)* Hey scaredy cats, why are you hiding in here?

FROGGY.   We're taking refuge from the sea of tackiness out there.

ZIP.   Hey, that's not —

POOKER.   Toasts in Italian. This is not the typical country club wedding.

ZIP.   Be nice, OK?

FROGGY.   *(In a burlesque Italian accent.)* Bambino a bambina. Eh!

POOKER.   *Bella, bella.*

FROGGY.   I'ma gonna propose a toasta. To the beautiful Chloe, who looksa just like Susan Lucci —

ZIP.   This isn't funny.

SOOS.   *(Enters.)* Froggy?

FROGGY.   Yes?

SOOS.   I think I hear your mom calling.

BRI.   We were just talking about how tacky Hutch's bride is.

ZIP.   Could you all, you know, just possibly try to be a little less venomous? I mean, so there is actually someone in the world who is different than us. I mean, I don't see this as a reason to — whatever.

POOKER.   We're just trashing. Relax. We're all just taken aback. I mean, there is seriously a man out there named Uncle Guido. *GUIDO* like, "Hello, Guido, what a lovely necklace … es."

FROGGY.   She's beneath him.

ZIP. Oh fuck.

FROGGY. What?

ZIP. People don't actually say things like that, do they?

FROGGY. I just did.

ZIP. Oh —

FROGGY. And I mean it. She's ... climbing. There. I've said it again. Out and out.

ZIP. I don't want to hear any more talk about Hutch. OK? He's a ... very close friend to me. And I don't think it's really cool for anyone to say anything about Chloe. She's a very sweet girl — lady. She's — she seems nice. So, I mean, she's probably just like one of us in a way.

FROGGY. She's wearing an ankle bracelet.

ZIP. This is all so petty.

SOOS. No, right. I think Zipper has a point. Let's all just chill. We should give Chloe the benefit of the doubt. She's probably very different from her family. I mean we're all different from our families. It's just a little disconcerting to have a full Italian wedding at the country club. That's all. I mean, even Wes Carpenter seems a little shaken. He's never had quite so many requests for "Arrivederci, Roma." But, I mean, hey, we might as well just go with it.

BRI. Shh. Here they come.

SOOS. I mean everyone has to be an outsider once.

BRI. Ixnay.

CHLOE. *(Entering with Hutch.)* Hey, you guys are missing all the fun.

FROGGY. Did Uncle Guido take his teeth out?

POOKER. Frogs.

CHLOE. We just did the tarantella.

HUTCH. The dance with the spinning.

POOKER. We saw that. Very ethnic.

FROGGY. Very *Godfather Part One*.

BRI. I took a course in folk dance in college. It was like that. *(Pause.)* It was only two credits.

CHLOE. I just came in to tell you we're ready to do the money basket!

SOOS. The money what?

CHLOE. It's a family tradition. Hutch and me get in the middle of the dance floor. I sit down and Hutch stands behind me, puts a basket on my head and all the guests circle us and throw cash in the basket to, you know, help out with expenses.

SOOS.   Oh.

CHLOE.   Doesn't it sound like fun?

FROGGY.   It sounds like white slavery.

CHLOE.   What?

BRI.   Louise.

FROGGY.   Nothing.

CHLOE.   You ready, let's go! Hurry!! *Andiamo! (Chloe and Hutch exit.)*

FROGGY.   Brian, love, hopefully the heavens will part and something will break them up.

POOKER.   Oh now, Froggers.

FROGGY.   Pardon me? Festive peasant dances? Eight-foot hoagies? Screw-top red wine bottles on the table? I think we're only a hop, skip and a jump away from bocci on the tennis courts. Jesus God, how I hope the heavens part. *(Pause.)* Well ... c'mon, Bri, let's go to the buffet and try to find some food that won't give us gas. *(She exits with Bri.)*

POOKER.   You coming, Soos?

SOOS.   Yeah, I'm on my way.

POOKER.   I'm going to sneak out. I have totally promised to do the chicken dance with Uncle Guido. If I keep a low profile, I might be able to dis that obligation. *(She exits.)*

ZIP.   Shit, how they love to bitch.

SOOS.   Hey everybody bitches. It's just to what degree.

ZIP.   You were like awfully supportive then.

SOOS.   You seemed alone. I hate that.

ZIP.   They just irritate me. You know, ragging on Hutch.

SOOS.   Yes. You're very loyal to Hutch.

ZIP.   Yeah. Sure. Of course.

SOOS.   And his bride.

ZIP.   *(Pause.)* And so are you.

SOOS.   She seems alone. As I said, I hate that. She looks ... somewhat alone. I used to think being alone was like strength-building. Now I think being alone is ... like the most hateful experience known to man. I don't like it. I —

ZIP.   Yes. She seems nice. I guess we should be going.

SOOS.   How are you doing these days, Zip?

ZIP.   I'm fine, why?

SOOS.   Nothing. No reason in particular. Do you know how I'm doing?

ZIP.   I'm sorry, I should have asked. How are you doing?

SOOS.   I'm fine. All's well. Nothing to complain about. I work nine to five at a job that is as intellectually taxing as, let's say, napping. Then I go home and have dinner with my parents where we discuss how my father's job is going. His makes mine look like a think tank. So we all drink some scotch. And then I go out and rent some bad movies. So I watch the movies and, if there were good parts, I rewind and watch them again. And when I'm alone and in bed and my life is no longer crowded with all this refreshing incident, I reflect on things. I just sit, smoke and, you know, kind of reflect. On things. Just … the way people behave. I just play back the interesting parts. Kind of like the movies that I rent. My life is pretty much a —

ZIP.   Then leave. Why don't you leave?

SOOS.   Because I've been here just long enough that the outside world seems frightening again.

ZIP.   Are you telling me this to like make me guilt-ridden or something?

SOOS.   Oh no. Oh, please. No, not at all. Of course not. I just — I want to tell you about my observation of you that I've been playing in my head. Like a rented movie.

ZIP.   An observation?

SOOS.   Just a bunch of things that you do that add up.

ZIP.   Yeah, like what?

SOOS.   Like … you're very protective of Chloe. (Pause.)

ZIP.   What does that mean?

SOOS.   What it means doesn't matter anymore. She's married to your best friend. So it's a little late.

ZIP.   What are you like insinuating here?

SOOS.   Nothing. Nothing will happen. You're not a fool. You have singles?

ZIP.   Singles? For what?

SOOS.   The money basket. C'mon, you'll be late.

ZIP. What are you saying?

SOOS. Meet you on the dance floor. *(She exits.)*

ZIP. I — what do you — I know what you're saying. What you're hinting at. And you're wrong. Real, real wrong. *(A pause. He shouts off after her.)* And I'm not a fool, OK? *(He runs after her.)*

Scene 7

"Independence Day"

Froggy has gone overboard with the decorations. Everyone is in summer whites. It would be a lovely day for a picnic if it weren't for the torrential downpour. Froggy, Bri, Pooker and Chloe are seated, bored, with beer cans in hand. Hutch, already wasted, rambles aimlessly around the cub room.

BRI. American League.

FROGGY. American way.

HUTCH. American ... woman.

FROGGY. What?

HUTCH. *(Sings.)* AMERICAN WOMAN, STAY AWAY FROM ME-HE. *(He plays air guitar.)*

FROGGY. This is a real prize you've married, Chloe. A real bad boy of rock 'n' roll.

CHLOE. *American in Paris.*

POOKER. American eagle.

FROGGY. American — uhm — American flag.

POOKER. American Express.

BRI. Uh — American Airlines.

CHLOE. Good one.

FROGGY. This is Morguesville, U.S.A.

POOKER. Frogwoman, we are intensely having a fine time. I know it's not what you planned, but —

FROGGY. You can't count on the weather.

CHLOE. My turn. American cheese.

FROGGY. I wanted a picnic. We worked hard for a picnic. *(Zip and Soos enter with a cooler full of beer.)*

ZIP. Beer here!

HUTCH. Yes!!

ZIP. And as a tribute to the Fourth of July, Froggy has only American beer.

HUTCH. Froggy, we salute you.

SOOS. Of course, it's in a Japanese cooler because the American cooler fell apart.

FROGGY. Ha ha. Very funny. Think of something American. Zip, your turn.

ZIP. American Tourister.

SOOS. *American Gothic.*

BRI. What?

SOOS. A painting.

FROGGY. They'll probably cancel the fireworks too. Fucking rain.

POOKER. American Indian.

BRI. Afro-American.

POOKER. Doesn't count. American has to be first.

BRI. OK. "American Pie."

HUTCH. Excellent.

ZIP. "Drove the Chevy to the levy but the levy was dry." Good call.

POOKER. I'm lost.

ZIP. It's a song. About Buddy Holly.

HUTCH. No, it's not, it's about James Dean.

FROGGY. Chloe, could you keep an eye on your husband. I think he's going to fall down.

HUTCH. It's James Dean. *(He falls down, then.)* Safe!

ZIP. Your turn, Chloe.

CHLOE. American Flyer.

ZIP. Uhm. OK American Dream.

HUTCH. James Dean.

CHLOE. Just ignore him.

BRI. What is the American Dream anyway?

POOKER. Really. I mean that is a total, you know, overworked

34

cliché that is so overused that it means like nada.

FROGGY. You work hard and plan and then it rains and you're left with a party that might as well not be a party. It might as well be a non-party day. A regular day.

POOKER. I mean truly, what does it mean?

SOOS. We're having fun. Don't worry, Froggy.

FROGGY. Hutch has passed out.

CHLOE. The American Dream means ... I mean who knows what it means now, but it started out meaning the like thing that everybody aspires to. The American Dream. Like having two kids and a house with a fence. And a car. What everyone wants. I think. *(Pause.)*

BRI. Oh. *(Pause.)* That's it?

POOKER. I thought it was more.

CHLOE. No. I think that's it. *(Pause.)*

BRI. I thought it was like bigger. Shit. I had all that when I was born. My parents had that. My grandparents had that.

SOOS. Same here. *(Pause.)*

BRI. Are you sure that's what it means?

CHLOE. Well ... yeah.

BRI. Shit. Another thing we're too late for. How many times does that happen, right?

POOKER. What?

BRI. Something important happens and we're too late for it. It's like everything that's important has happened before us. I feel that I was late for the Sixties. Just being born and all. Protesting and shit? I would have done it. I would have been a real, you know, vigorous rebel against Vietnam. I would have hated Vietnam. I would have carried a sign. No sweat. If there were a Vietnam-like situation today, I would protest. I would sing songs with a guitar. Grow my hair long. Make peace signs. And just, you know ... hate the establishment and stuff. Where's the dip?

ZIP. Aren't there Vietnam-like situations now?

BRI. I don't think so. I think we'd know about it.

ZIP. Brian, we've invaded quite a few countries since Vietnam.

BRI. Yes, but wars now are so short. By the time you figure out which side you're on, they're long over. I mean Vietnam was long enough to be so black and white. You knew what to be angry about.

Wars now are like bright gray. The really good angry is gone.

POOKER.   Civil rights, like.

BRI.   Exactly. Civil rights. Case in fucking point. I would have been a champion of civil rights. Separate counters and such? Oh I would have been so against it, it wouldn't even be funny. I would have marched with Martin Luther ... King. But all that's ... said and done. I mean there is inequality and stuff all over the world. Racial whatnot. I'm not blind. But it's all over there. In ... whattayacall?

FROGGY.   Kosovo. Pass the nuts.

BRI.   Kosovo. It's none of our business. For protest and rage and stuff? We're just too late. Face it.

ZIP.   You're joking, right?

BRI.   No, why?

ZIP.   Well, for starters you're in a restricted country club talking civil rights. Doesn't that make you feel a little ... doesn't it make any of you feel a little — you know, just because we sit here at the club while the country is falling to shit doesn't mean we have to be in denial and whatnot. Passion and rage are always with us. I think you should always have things to hate and to ... love. They're both out there. And.

SOOS.   When did you come up with this philosophy?

ZIP.   I don't know. It's just things. Things happen and ... Nothing. Nothing has happened. It's just a — let's play the game. American. *American Werewolf in London.*

HUTCH.   James Dean.

SOOS.   Hutch, we are no longer talking about the Don McLean song.

BRI.   I don't know, Zip. Everything is so OK now. So, I mean, to be upset about anything would be like a waste of time.

POOKER.   Hutch has passed out.

CHLOE.   He'll wake up.

FROGGY.   This isn't what I planned. I planned a very special party. Something special and different. But it rained.

SOOS.   That's OK. It's nothing to get upset about.

FROGGY.   Dr. Brooker says that I have to sublimate my feelings of terror into an activity, so I sublimate my feelings of terror into putting these parties together and I'm getting no help and — Bri?

BRI. Yes.

FROGGY. Why don't we do something spontaneous?

BRI. No.

FROGGY. Why don't we move the party to our house?

BRI. There's no room.

FROGGY. I mean my parents' house.

CHLOE. On Old Mill Road?

FROGGY. Yes.

CHLOE. Nice.

FROGGY. The martini pool. It will be frivolous. We could break into my parents' bar.

CHLOE. I think this is great.

POOKER. Are we seriously going to break into someone's parents' bar?

SOOS. I know. I've been on the planet for three decades. Why does this fill me with such joy?

ZIP. Hutch! Wake up!!

HUTCH. James Dean.

ZIP. Hutch, wake up. We're going to go get some booze at Froggy's.

HUTCH. It's James Dean! James Dean! James Dean!! *(He suddenly freaks out. Soos and Zip calm him by holding him gently. Soos then states clearly and soothingly.)*

SOOS. Hutch, it's not James Dean. There's a line in the song that says something like, "I remember the day he died, How his widow cried and cried." James Dean did not have a widow. The song doesn't say, "I remember the day he died, How Sal Mineo cried and cried." Now, please get up so you can go with us to Froggy's.

HUTCH. I'm getting up.

FROGGY. Bri and I will take him, OK?

CHLOE. Great. *(Froggy and Bri help Hutch to stand up. They then support him.)*

POOKER. You need a ride, Soos?

SOOS. Sure. Fine.

HUTCH. James Dean!

BRI. We'll take Hutch. Who's going to take Chloe?

37

POOKER.   You want to go with us?

ZIP.   I'm going. Why don't you go with me?

POOKER.   That's good. Go with Zip. Soos and I can stop for cigs.

FROGGY.   Great. Pooker and Soos. Zip and Chloe. Now, Chloe, don't worry. We have your husband.

SOOS.   Sounds like a kidnapping. *(Pooker and Soos exit.)*

HUTCH.   James Dean!!

FROGGY.   Shhhh.

HUTCH.   I used to look like James Dean.

FROGGY.   You never looked like James Dean.

HUTCH.   I did. Now I look like a country club drunk.

FROGGY.   That's silly. What does a country club drunk look like?

HUTCH.   Me. Hey, Chloe! You coming with?

CHLOE.   No room in the car. I'm gong with Zip.

HUTCH.   Hooray for Zip!

FROGGY.   Hooray for Zip.

HUTCH.   I love Zip. Do you love Zip?

BRI.   What's not to love?

FROGGY.   Hutch never looked like James Dean. *(Froggy and Bri carry Hutch out. Chloe and Zip are left alone. There is an awkward pause. Neither knows exactly what to say.)*

ZIP.   I'm just going to — why don't you finish your drink?

CHLOE.   I've had enough.

ZIP.   Oh. *(Pause.)* Well, then why are you going to Froggy's?

CHLOE.   Oh, uh, I don't know. Everyone seems to be going and —

ZIP.   And?

CHLOE.   It's on Old Mill Road. You ever seen the inside of a house on Old Mill Road?

ZIP.   Sure. Since I was, what? Three.

CHLOE.   Some of us weren't never "what? Three." Some of us were — never mind. I think we should be going.

ZIP.   Oh. Why?

CHLOE.   I don't know. You're staring at me. It gives me the willies.

ZIP.   Sorry.

CHLOE.   You do it a lot.

ZIP.   I won't. *(He looks away. Then looks back.)* Sorry.

CHLOE.   You're staring at me like everybody's staring at me on account of you think I'm a climber.

ZIP.   I don't — a wha —

CHLOE.   A climber. That frog lady person I overhear her in the ladies' telling somebody I'm a climber. You think I'm a climber.

ZIP.   I'm not sure I know exactly — no. Not in the least. *(He leans in and kisses her. They have a long passionate kiss, then stare at one another for a moment.)*

CHLOE.   Where did that —

ZIP.   Sorry. I am —

CHLOE.   Locomotion behavior —

ZIP.   So sorry.

CHLOE.   Come fro — that's — I don't know what to say to that.

ZIP.   I — I'm smitten. I've been smitten for a while.

CHLOE.   *(Moving away from him.)* Stay there. I got married to a perfectly nice — I got a ring and I don't —

ZIP.   What are you saying.

CHLOE.   I'm saying, "Stop." "Zip, stop." I'm saying, "Leave me alone." Just … let's go. Let's just go. Let's go to Froggy's parents and have fun and stop coming towards me.

ZIP.   I'm in pain.

CHLOE.   Stop.

ZIP.   I am hurting, as in torture.

CHLOE.   Fucking up my life.

ZIP.   It's like knives are sticking in me.

CHLOE.   Don't kiss me. Please don't kiss me. *(She grabs his face and kisses him full on the lips.)*

END OF ACT ONE

ACT TWO

Scene 1

"Labor Day"

No music. A dim blue light comes from one of the windows and vaguely reveals a nude couple huddled in a blanket. It is only as they speak that we realize that it is Zip and Chloe.

CHLOE. Hey.
ZIP. What?
CHLOE. Happy Labor Day.
ZIP. Shit.
CHLOE. Ha.
ZIP. That was —
CHLOE. Oh God.
ZIP. Really kind of —
CHLOE. It was.
ZIP. Spectacular. That was spectacular.
CHLOE. And athletic. It was athletic. And. And full of pleasure. I mean it was on a hardwood floor, but still it was pleasure. And —
ZIP. Yes?
CHLOE. It was ... silly. We better go.
ZIP. Stay.
CHLOE. I gotta go.
ZIP. Please stay. A little longer.
CHLOE. I'll have a cigarette.
ZIP. Have a cigarette.
CHLOE. Thanks for suggesting it. *(She pulls out a cigarette and lights it. Zip laughs to himself.)* What are you laughing at.

ZIP.   It *WAS* kind of silly.

CHLOE.   Yes. Ah! *(She slaps a bug off the back of her neck.)* Bugs are coming in. I'm gonna light a citronella. *(Chloe finds a citronella candle and lights it.)*

ZIP.   Don't move.

CHLOE.   *(Frozen.)* What?

ZIP.   *(Gently.)* Don't move.

CHLOE.   What's the matter?

ZIP.   Nothing. Just the way you look right now. It's so tremendous.

CHLOE.   Oh that. I though you saw a bug or something.

ZIP.   Stay there a second. With the candle. You're like incredible. With the candlelight on your face and neck. And the moonlight which is kind of dancing in your hair. It should be a picture. A pretentious picture in black and white. *Chloe by Candlelight.* And it would hang in a gallery in New York City. And everyone who had seen all kinds of beautiful pictures would think that this was the most beautiful of all. *Chloe by Candlelight.* Lots of New York people with goop in their hairs would look at your picture and burst into tears and remark at its beauty.

CHLOE.   Oh God. You just don't turn it off.

ZIP.   What?

CHLOE.   The gushing thing you do.

ZIP.   Am I laying it on too thick for you?

CHLOE.   Be realistic, it's not the moonlight that's dancing in my hair it's the light from the bug zapper.

ZIP.   Oh. Well. It's the thought that counts.

CHLOE.   What we just did … on the hardwood floor … was enough. You don't got to work at complimenting me.

ZIP.   It's not something I'm working. I'm speaking from my heart. Like.

CHLOE.   Oh. OK. That's different. *(Pause.)* We should be going.

ZIP.   I don't want tonight to end.

CHLOE.   Tonight ended. We're into today.

ZIP.   Ahhhh.

CHLOE.   Let's go.

ZIP.   Why don't you lay down beside me and I'll put my arm

41

around you and I'll breathe on your hair and you can tell me things?

CHLOE. *(Awkwardly trying to handle her blanket and her lit cigarette, she begins to look for her clothing.)* We gotta leave.

ZIP. Why?

CHLOE. Because it's Labor Day. Everyone will be coming soon to set up for the picnic. Hutch and his dad'll be back from fishing.

ZIP. Stay with me.

CHLOE. I can't

ZIP. Aren't you happy with me?

CHLOE. Yes, of course. I mean, you care so much about us. I mean, the fact that you would remember our two-month anniversary and suggest that we go to the very spot where we met and make love, for me shows a big amount of creative energy ... I'm so touched. But, I mean, I can't go on like this.

ZIP. Oh, shit. Why?

CHLOE. It's a sin. *(Zip laughs.)* Yeah. Ho ho. Real funny. You don't know about sin. You Methodists or whatever you all are act like sin is ... a stroke you missed on the golf course or something. I was brought up right. A sin is something. And this is a sin, whether or not it is mortal or venial I cannot tell you. I just should get myself to a confessional with a priest that don't know my Aunt Gina and find out. Where's my bra?

ZIP. You weren't wearing one. Stay with me.

CHLOE. I don't want to go to hell, do you mind?

ZIP. There is no hell. Only people in love. That's the only hell.

CHLOE. You'll feel different when you're dead. Where are my socks?

ZIP. You weren't wearing any.

CHLOE. And if we're looking for a perfect farewell — and I am — I think this is a real nice book-end kind of ending. Did I have stockings on?

ZIP. No.

CHLOE. And the lovemaking — not the sex. I really consider it lovemaking — that we just did-had-made-whatever was the best in my life. So I —

ZIP. It was?

CHLOE. So I think —

ZIP. Really?

CHLOE. Don't let it go to your head. So, I mean, that's a perfect memory. On the hardwood floor. And when I'm looking back on this — all right I'm going to say the word — fling, I can remember this particular moment on the hard wood floor with nostalgia. And I'll pray for forgiveness. Where are my panties?

ZIP. You weren't wearing any.

CHLOE. What did we leave to get here? A burning building?

ZIP. We left a dinner at Stokesay. *(A moment. She remembers the dinner with fondness.)*

CHLOE. Yes. I enjoyed that, thank you. I think maybe you should get dressed.

ZIP. *(He gets up and puts on his underwear.)* Well, I don't mean to be negative right now, but I think … I mean, don't you think it kind of says something that the relationship is over not five seconds and you're looking for lovely memories already? Aren't you thinking you're making a mistake? I don't think you're thinking ahead.

CHLOE. Of course I'm thinking ahead.

ZIP. No I —

CHLOE. I'm thinking ahead more than you are.

ZIP. How can you say that?

CHLOE. Because I am a woman and women think ahead more than men.

ZIP. Men think ahead.

CHLOE. Men rarely think beyond their next ejaculation.

ZIP. Whoa. *(A pause.)*

CHLOE. So just stop talking and get … just get dressed.

ZIP. *(As they finish getting dressed.)* Next ejacula — where did that come from? I think ahead. *(Pause. He stops getting dressed.)* OK OK.

CHLOE. What?

ZIP. OK. Let's run off.

CHLOE. What?

ZIP. Let's get in my car and drive until we find a town that we both have never heard of and get drunk on cheap wine and play some Sam Cooke and make love all the time and start a life together.

CHLOE.   Why would we want to do something like that?

ZIP.   Because we love each other.

CHLOE.   We don't —

ZIP.   We do we do. We just don't know it because we're both in denial because you're a Catholic and I'm a Republican and denial is like the first response for us. *(She smiles.)* You're smiling. Let's get married.

CHLOE.   No.

ZIP.   No? Just no?

CHLOE.   Yes. No.

ZIP.   Do I, you know, get a how come?

CHLOE.   I'm already married to somebody else. *(Pause. She turns the light on.)* Thanks for the offer though. It was sweet. If you're looking for your Top-Siders, they're over there.

ZIP.   When will I see you again?

CHLOE.   Later today. The picnic.

ZIP.   No. I mean *SEE* you.

CHLOE.   I swear to God you are brain-damaged. I won't see you again. We ended. Very nice. When I'm with you … it's getting to be too much.

ZIP.   It's over?

CHLOE.   It's over, let's go.

ZIP.   Just like that?

CHLOE.   It was a great ending. Let's go.

ZIP.   It was a great farewell.

CHLOE.   Yes.

ZIP.   The making love on the very spot where we met. It was a perfect ending.

CHLOE.   Yes.

ZIP.   You wouldn't have it any other way.

CHLOE.   *(Suspiciously.)* We're going somewhere with this.

ZIP.   Only … maybe I'm wrong, but I think … wasn't it over here … where we met? *(A pause. She considers it. She walks over to the spot. Examines it. She looks at him. She drops the blanket on the spot and walks over to the light.)*

CHLOE.   I think you're right. *(She turns off the overhead light. In the blue light she walks over to him and they begin to make love as the lights slowly go to black.)*

44

Scene 2

"Halloween"

Soos, dressed as the Queen of Hearts, is looking out the window. Pooker, dressed as a witch, is stretched out on the sofa reading an issue of Town and Country.

POOKER.   I mean, as pagan rituals go, this has got to be one of the dullest. I mean, it is of such non-interest. *(Pause.)* I don't know if Froggy is like to blame or anything. I think we're all over each other. I'm almost glad some people are wearing masks tonight. If I actually saw their faces again, I might scream. *(Pause.)* I never want to go to another party again.

SOOS.   Oop. There goes Tarzan with Cinderella into the pool house.

POOKER.   What?

SOOS.   Tarzan and Cinderella just snuck out of the club to the pool house.

POOKER.   Great. I hope they have fun.

SOOS.   You think?

POOKER.   Do I think what?

SOOS.   That they're off ... having fun.

POOKER.   Oh please. Of course.

SOOS.   Oh. *(Pause.)* I wonder how Frankenstein feels about that?

POOKER.   Who is Frankenstein?

SOOS.   Cinderella's husband.

POOKER.   Soos?

SOOS.   Yeah?

POOKER.   Stop.

SOOS.   Stop what?

POOKER.   Stop referring to everyone by their costumes.

SOOS.   Oh.

POOKER. *(Suddenly swings open the door and shouts.)* I'm bored!!! *(Just as suddenly, she closes the door and says in her normal voice.)* Froggy's catching on. She's getting but frantic with the party games. *(A sudden realization.)* Hey, wait a minute! I think ... that I ... am bored. *(Mock light laughter.)*

SOOS. I wonder how long that's been going on.

POOKER. About two hours. I've been bored since the hokey-pokey.

SOOS. No, the affair between Cinderella and Tarzan.

POOKER. Soos?

SOOS. Yes?

POOKER. Eighty-six the costume names.

SOOS. Sorry. Chloe and Zip. I wonder how long Chloe and Zip have been having an affair.

POOKER. Seriously. Don't you think Froggy has been going but nuts with the activities? I swear, these parties are beginning to feel like Montessori day care.

SOOS. How long do you think Zip and Chloe have been having an affair?

POOKER. Really. Look, this candy is shaped like a ghost. I'm going to eat it.

SOOS. Pook?

POOKER. What?

SOOS. Answer my question.

POOKER. I thought it was rhetorical.

SOOS. It's not. Answer it.

POOKER. I don't know. A couple of months.

SOOS. Well.

POOKER. A while, anyway. This magazine is so banal.

SOOS. Well now. I didn't know that.

POOKER. I swear to God their writers are like in the REM state when they're doing these articles.

SOOS. That's interesting.

POOKER. What's interesting?

SOOS. Zip is sleeping with Chloe.

POOKER. Why is that interesting?

SOOS. Because it hurts me.

POOKER. What, didn't you know?

SOOS. I mean, I was suspicious. But ... no.

POOKER. Don't let it hurt you. Look at the people in these party pictures. They're excessively gleeful.

SOOS. I think I'm going to tell Frankenstein. Hutch is Frankenstein.

POOKER. You do and I'll kick you in the head.

SOOS. Why?

POOKER. Because it's none of your business.

SOOS. But Chloe is sleeping with Zip.

POOKER. So?

SOOS. Well, I mean, that's something.

POOKER. Chloe is sleeping with Zip, Barb is in love with Mitch Williams, Mitch Williams is gay, P.J. keeps attempting suicide over Prescott, I have a boyfriend that isn't cute whom I love, Sketchy is bankrupt, Icky has cancer, Froggy is filled with terror, Hutch is a drunk, Bri has an ulcer, Ginny has a mixed marriage that's on the rocks, Bags is frequenting prostitutes, and you're never leaving Wyomissing, no matter how much you say you are. We all have our little stories. And no one brings them up. That's what's known as community spirit.

SOOS. Oh.

POOKER. So don't even think of like broaching the subject.

SOOS. OK.

POOKER. Have some candy corn.

SOOS. I don't know. I can go either way with candy corn.

POOKER. Yeah, me too. *(Pause.)* Shit. Look at this house. I am like green with envy over this house. This is the most stunning, big, beautiful house. *(Soos begins to cry.)* I could be oh so happy in a house this size. I would have parties. Parties of the damned. I could have parties and entertain really flawless people and — *(Pause.)* Come look at this house, Soos. You'll die. *(Pause.)* Soos? *(Pause. Pooker looks up for the first time.)* You crying, Soos?

SOOS. Oh, please.

Scene 3

"Thanksgiving"

The entire company is seated and stuffed from overeating. Everyone still has a coffee mug. Soos has a bottle of Asti. There is laughter.

ZIP.   Donna pulls out this joint the size of an adult male arm.

HUTCH.   We were driving out past Robesonia. Out in Amish country.

ZIP.   And we were all toking on this bone.

BRI.   Louise toked a joint?!

FROGGY.   This was in high school. Think of me as a different person.

ZIP.   So we were all buzzed. Real buzzed. And we're seeing all these Amish people. Buggy after buggy of Amish people. With their beards and old-fashioned hats. And the women in their long dresses.

SOOS.   Asti, anyone?

ZIP.   And Hutch sees like this hundredth buggy go by and no cars and he starts to get totally paranoid.

HUTCH.   I get so paranoid when I smoke pot. That's why I gave it up.

SOOS.   May we change the subject?

ZIP.   And he's suddenly confused as to what century we're in. He says all he's been seeing is people from the eighteen hundreds, so it must be the eighteen hundreds. And he's complaining so loud and so long that after a while he starts to make sense.

FROGGY.   We were so wasted.

ZIP.   So we decided to pull over and ask this buggy full of Amish people what century it was. Only we kind of pulled over a little too directly. And we slammed into the buggy and the horse ran over the hood and — *(Zip, Froggy and Hutch laugh.)*

48

SOOS.   Chloe, Bri, I really don't think you want to hear about "S.D. at the convent."
CHLOE.   Nah. It's interesting.
ZIP.   And we're like, whoa. This is too exhilarating for words. So we get the hell out of there — you know it's the only time I ever heard an Amish man say "Fuck You!"
HUTCH.   I think it was more "Fuck Thou."
ZIP.   Ha! And we are so hot and sweaty and we all decide we should go somewhere for a swim and cool off.
HUTCH.   Now this was still spring so the club and the public pool were closed.
ZIP.   And Wyomissing creek —
FROGGY.   Not even a consideration.
ZIP.   So Donna tells us about this convent. How she knew about a convent, I don't know.
FROGGY.   Stang!!!!
ZIP.   So she takes us to the convent, we jump over the fence and —
HUTCH.   Tell 'em how we parked the car.
ZIP.   That's not interesting.
HUTCH.   You're right.
ZIP.   So we get to the pool and the water is nice and cold.
FROGGY.   Keep an open mind, Bri. Remember, I was a troubled youth.
ZIP.   Now the pool is just like a regular pool — shallow to deep — except where the diving board ought to be there's this Virgin Mary.
POOKER.   Do the nuns jump off of that?
ZIP.   Nah. I don't think nuns are allowed to dive. So this statue is just standing there like this — *(He strikes the pose of a Virgin Mary. Both hands out at the side.)*
HUTCH.   No, it wasn't, it was like this — *(He strikes another Virgin Mary pose. This one with one arm extended at the waist, the other hand on the heart.)*
ZIP.   Get real, she was like this. *(Emphasizes his pose.)*
HUTCH.   No way, she was like — *(He emphasizes his pose.)*
ZIP.   She was like this and her face was complacent.
HUTCH.   No, her face was mournful. She had her hand over

her heart.

ZIP.   Froggy, you were there, which was it?

FROGGY.   I'm afraid Hutch is right. It was the hand-on-the-heart mournful variety.

ZIP.   Well anyway, there's this Madonna at the pool who you can't dive off.

CHLOE.   Guys, could we lay off the B.V.M. stuff?

SOOS.   You think you're offended now, wait.

ZIP.   And Donna starts acting very crazy when she sees this statue. She starts crying and praying for forgiveness and falling on her knees and praying and —

HUTCH.   It was crying weed. And she was Catholic.

SOOS.   Anybody offended yet? The story's young.

ZIP.   Well, suddenly in like one fell swoop, she takes off all of her clothes and jumps into the pool. We are like flabbergasted. But it was all so free and impressive that we all followed suit.

POOKER.   Or you followed without suits.

ZIP.   Right.

POOKER.   "S.D. at the convent." Skinny-dipping at the convent.

CHLOE.   I get it.

POOKER.   Too funny.

ZIP.   And we're having a real giddy time. Laughing and splashing and losing ourselves and —

HUTCH.   And playing —

HUTCH and FROGGY.   Water polo!

ZIP.   And suddenly these like searchlights go off.

FROGGY.   *(Laughing.)* Oh shit. *(Froggy and Hutch begin to act things out.)*

ZIP.   And these like vicious nuns come out. Really worked up. With big sticks.

HUTCH.   Brooms.

ZIP.   Right, brooms.

HUTCH.   And they're chasing us and screaming and swinging these brooms and yelling, "Shame, shame, shame!"

FROGGY.   *(Imitating a nun.)* Shame, shame, shame.

ZIP.   And they called the police.

HUTCH.   Because there was sirens. We knew the police were

50

coming because we heard sirens. It was a real madhouse. The lights, the sirens, the nuns —

ZIP.   And one of these killer nuns has Hutch pinned against the wall swinging her broom. And Hutch, who was just so trapped, just suddenly started growling at her. And she looks at him up and down and she says —

ZIP and FROGGY.   "Oh dear Lord, it's a bear!" *(All except Soos laugh.)*

ZIP.   And she runs away.

SOOS.   She probably said, "Oh dear Lord, he's bare."

ZIP.   No. No. I know for a fact it was, "Oh dear Lord, it's a bear."

SOOS.   You have the most selective memory. Offended yet, Chloe?

CHLOE.   No. Nuns are OK. I just don't like B.V.M. jokes.

ZIP.   So we ran the hell out of there not even having time to put clothes on or anything. And we rode off in the car laughing and singing and loving life and not having clothes on.

HUTCH.   So anyway, Zip and Froggy are in Trig class.

BRI.   You're still naked?

SOOS.   No. We go now to the fall of the senior year. This is where we hand out the vomit bags.

ZIP.   So, Froggy and I are in Trig class. And Mr. Burke, who is chairman of the yearbook, calls me into his room. And he says, "Zipper, I'm looking over the write-up here that you want to go next to your senior picture and under memorable events you wrote 'S.D. at the convent'. Now, you know Zipper how we feel about initials".

FROGGY.   They were totally wigged out by people putting initials in the yearbook ever since they found out some of the initials were drug-related terms.

ZIP.   And he said to me, "Is 'S.D. at the convent' ... Does the 'S.D.' stand for ... a drug-related term?" And he was so sad and sincere that I had to chew on the inside of my mouth not to crack up.

HUTCH.   Then tell them what you did. This is genius.

SOOS.   The genius that is Zip.

ZIP.   So —

SOOS.   I'm finishing the Asti.

ZIP.   Just off the top of my head. I suddenly looked offended and

51

I said, "Mr. Burke. I'll have you know that 'S.D.' stands for 'sincere devotion.'" *(All except Soos laugh.)*

HUTCH. Sincere devotions at the convent! *(All except Soos laugh some more.)*

FROGGY. And he bought it! *(All except Soos laugh uproariously.)*

ZIP. And he — and he — no wait — and he got all embarrassed so I just laid it on about how if the other students knew that I prayed they'd all make fun of me so I put it in initials but I had to put it in my write-up because it was so important to me but if he wants me to remove it I certainly will and he's like, "No, no, no, no" … *(All except Soos laugh.)*

SOOS. And now the moral.

FROGGY. There's no moral, it's just a funny funny story.

HUTCH. *(With admiration.)* The moral is that Zip is one hell of a fucking dancer. He dances his way out of everything.

SOOS. The moral — if the word "moral" can be used in context with that story — strikes me as being a little more profound.

BRI. Oh, Soos, what are you talking "profound"? This is just Zip.

FROGGY. What do you mean?

SOOS. To me the moral would be, "Getting away with it is an illusion."

FROGGY. What?

ZIP. How would that —

SOOS. Because Zip, in your selective memory, you forgot to tell everyone an important moment at the convent.

ZIP. No, I —

SOOS. That night at the convent, before you went "S.D.ing," you porked Donna.

HUTCH. *(In an explosion of laughter.)* Faced!! *(All laugh.)*

ZIP. *(With a laugh.)* I did? Was that then? Oh, God. I forgot.

SOOS. Yes, you did. I know because Froggy and Hutch watched you.

HUTCH. Yeah, that I remember.

SOOS. And you were going out with me at the time. And Froggy, the original P.A. system, ran quicker than the speed of sound to tell me. About the porking and the skinny-dipping.

ZIP. That's right. I was going out with you back then. Isn't it funny the things that we remember and the things that we —

SOOS. And I denied it to the hilt saying, "Oh, no, there's no way he'd have sex with Donna. He's my boyfriend." And then that fall, when I was proofing the yearbook and I saw "S.D. at the convent" next to your heavily retouched picture, I knew that it was true.

FROGGY. Isn't that interesting? There's a whole 'nother side of the story. I'm in the mood for dessert. *(Mixed groans and cheers. Except Soos, who's still on it.)* Now, we have an apple pie which has a sour cream layer and a brown sugar crust. Yum yum. And there's a peach buckle and —

SOOS. Zip got away with it with Mr. Burke, but he didn't get away with it with me.

POOKER. Soos.

FROGGY. And a New York cheesecake.

BRI. Too many choices.

HUTCH. I'm going to bust.

SOOS. But I mean, that's so Zip isn't it?

FROGGY. We're talking about dessert now.

SOOS. Thinking he's getting away with a little adventure when he's not.

FROGGY. We're no longer talking about morals, we're talking about dessert.

SOOS. I wonder if the same holds true today.

POOKER. Soos. Stop it now. Please.

SOOS. If you know what I mean. If you get my D-R-I-F-T drift. If you know what I mean.

HUTCH. *(Calmly.)* We know what you mean, Soos. Now why don't you sit down and shut the fuck up? *(Shocked silence for a moment.)*

SOOS. *(Shattered.)* Oh ... I'm sorry ... Hutch, I ... I — *(She runs off.)*

FROGGY. Uh ... and the rest ... there's this real beautiful chocolate cake. And the ... There's some —

POOKER. *(Running off.)* Soos?

FROGGY. Peach buckle and I said that. And just lots of things. And a blueberry crepe thingie. Kind of thing. It's a —

HUTCH. *(Getting up.)* That's what I'll be having. You coming with, Bri? *(He exits.)*

BRI. Oh. Yeah. Sure. *(He stands by the door.)*

FROGGY. And there's — there are these baked cinnamon apples that are really — *(She looks at Chloe and Zip.)* Oh God. They have like a caramel, something like —

BRI. Come on, Froggy.

FROGGY. Louise. I'm on my way. *(Bri escorts Froggy off. Only Chloe and Zip are left. There's a moment of awkward silence. He walks toward her. He's about to say something.)*

CHLOE. And all my friends, my friends back on Reed Street, they ask me, "What's it like at the country club with all those country club snobs who got no heart and got no soul?" And I say, "No they're fine, they're just like you or me." *(Her words build in exhilaration.)* But the truth, the fucking truth, is you ain't, you people ain't like anybody, you got no soul, you got no heart, you got no God, no hell, no saints, no sin, no wrong, no sin, *(With each "no," she strikes Zip.)* no pain, no Jesus, no Mother of Jesus, no sin, no guilt, no hell, no hell, no hell. I hate you. *(She cries. He goes to comfort. She steps away and regains her composure.)* That's it. No. I mean, this is it. It is over as of this second.

ZIP. I —

CHLOE. Don't try. It's a waste of breath. It went on too long as is. Now everyone knows. Or to be more exact now we know that everyone knows. God only knows how long they've known or how long Hutch has known. *(It dawns on her what she has just said. She looks scared. She begins to cry.)* Oh God.

ZIP. Shit. Don't cry. *(He goes to comfort her. She moves away. She starts to leave, but stops at the door. She doesn't look at him.)*

CHLOE. I'm not crying. No one is going to see me cry. *(She exits. Zip stands alone on stage for a moment. He then says the only thing that has ever made sense.)*

ZIP. *(Quietly.)* But I love you.

Scene 4

"Christmas"

The lights come up on a very Yuletide cub room. Standing alone, Soos is drinking from a tall glass. Zip enters.

ZIP.   Pook, I — *(Spotting Soos.)* Oh.
SOOS.   Zip?
ZIP.   Uhm, hi. *(Turns to go.)*
SOOS.   Merry Christmas.
ZIP.   Yes. Right. Merry Christmas.
SOOS.   Zip, there's something I want to say to you.
ZIP.   Oh, I think you said enough last Thanksgiving, don't you?
SOOS.   Zip, please don't be confrontational, I'm not dressed for it.
ZIP.   I think I should leave.
SOOS.   Zip, please, be nice. I'm like real fragile here.
ZIP.   Sorry.
SOOS.   And. I want to apologize to you.
ZIP.   You don't have to —
SOOS.   I want to apologize for ruining stuff with you and Chloe and embarrassing you and —
ZIP.   It's all right, Soos. I accept your apology.
SOOS.   I'm sorry. I'm truly sorry.
ZIP.   I know, I know.
SOOS.   So Hutch and Chloe are …
ZIP.   Second honeymoon? Then moving away. I guess. Or back here. Maybe.
SOOS.   I'm sorry. *(Pause.)* Want some of my drink?
ZIP.   What are you drinking?
SOOS.   Rum and Coke. Serious girl drink. Are you man enough?
ZIP.   Sure. *(Takes Soos' glass and has a sip. A moment.)*
SOOS.   Mad at me?

ZIP. How could I be mad at you? We've been friends since like Hector was a pup. Whoever Hector is.

SOOS. Some dog, I guess. *(A pause.)* Oh, Zip.

ZIP. Oh, Soos.

SOOS. Oh, Zip and Soos.

ZIP. Whatever happened to Zip and Soos?

SOOS. Really.

ZIP. They started out with such promise. Such the hopes for tomorrow.

SOOS. Such the hopes.

ZIP. Such the lives we were going to lead.

SOOS. Such the lives. We were going to be so happy and successful and shit.

ZIP. And we were going to get married.

SOOS. Oh please. Of course. No question.

ZIP. Class president and class secretary? Dating all through junior and senior year? Marriage was like imminent.

SOOS. I mean, we went to separate colleges, but everyone knew. We were going to return to Wyo.

ZIP. To what? What did they want for us? Fuck. What did we want for us? Shit.

SOOS. I guess the whole happy marriage and successful business thing. I don't know, what did you want?

ZIP. Me? An office, I guess. An office of my own. In Reading. With my name on the door. Stenciled on the glass.

SOOS. A name on the door. Something to be proud of.

ZIP. It's all I ever wanted. Back when dreams were a consideration.

SOOS. What else?

ZIP. Did I want?

SOOS. Yeah.

ZIP. Three secretaries. To say goodbye to at the end of the day. Good night, girls. *(Imitating a secretary.)* Good night, Mr. Mueller. *(Imitating another secretary.)* Good night, Mr. Mueller. *(Imitating a voluptuous secretary.)* Good night, Mr. Mueller.

SOOS. More about that third secretary, please.

ZIP. Blonde. Stacked. Wants me. But can't have me because —

SOOS. What?

ZIP. I am —

SOOS. Uh-oh.

ZIP. Loyal —

SOOS. No.

ZIP. To my wife … Soos.

SOOS. God, how we talked about that.

ZIP. And we live happily ever after.

SOOS. It's too funny.

ZIP. In a house on the Boulevard.

SOOS. Which one?

ZIP. The Victorian white clapboard. The Gordon's old house.

SOOS. The house that made Martha Stewart forget she was Polish.

ZIP. Right. And secretary number three licks her lip and looks at my crotch but I say, "No no. I've got to get back to my Victorian white clapboard house on the Boulevard."

SOOS. That your wife has lovingly decorated in non-aggressive colors.

ZIP. And to my wife.

SOOS. Thank you, dear. Bring home some eggs.

ZIP. And to my two-point-five children.

SOOS. Two boys named —

ZIP. Morgan?

SOOS. Nice.

ZIP. And Chase.

SOOS. Those aren't sons, those are banks.

ZIP. And I drive home in my faithfully restored woody station wagon.

SOOS. Every man has a hobby, that's my Zipper's.

ZIP. And I drive home from the crime and Puerto Ricans of Reading to the beautiful green lawns and dormitory-looking single-family dwellings of Wyomissing. And I reflect on my life and I am … proud. Bursting with pride over the money I've made that day. Proud that the name Mueller means something in Berks County. Proud that my car and my house are such beautifully restored classics. Proud of my boys. Proud that my wife has a career and is still actively involved with volunteer work.

SOOS.   Throw pillows for the homeless.

ZIP.   And I'm proud of my stocks, and I'm proud of my holdings. And I'm proud that I can still get an erection when secretary number three flirts with me.

SOOS.   Eyes on the road dear.

ZIP.   And proud of the dinner my wife has prepared for me and the two boys waiting for me.

SOOS.   Boys, your father will be home soon, come sit at the table. Morgan Guarantee sit up. And stop pulling Chase Manhattan's hair. And Brandy, get off the sofa.

ZIP.   Who's Brandy? Our point-five child?

SOOS.   No, Brandy is our shedding, drooling and ill-trained golden retriever who's just like family.

ZIP.   Honey, I'm home.

SOOS.   How was your day at work, dear?

ZIP.   I made more money than anybody else and I have the respect of the community and I've been asked to be the Republican nominee for vice president of the United States. I'm so proud of myself. What's for dinner?

SOOS.   Swiss steaks.

ZIP.   What *ARE* Swiss steaks?

SOOS.   I don't know, but I made them. Morgan Guarantee stop pulling on Daddy's arm! Morgan Guarantee is very excited. He's going to be taking dance classes and he's entirely heterosexual. And little Chase Manhattan is equally excited because he's just finished writing his first short story. And he's in the third grade. And it's going to be published in *The New Yorker*.

ZIP.   The ultimate WASP dream. Creative children. How's my puppy, Brandy?

SOOS.   Brandy is writing a tone poem.

ZIP.   Creative pets! My heart is full. I'm so proud.

SOOS.   I'm so proud.

ZIP.   I am so proud.

SOOS.   We are so proud.

ZIP.   Wife, of whom I am so proud?

SOOS.   Yes, my pride-inducing husband?

ZIP.   May I ask you?

SOOS. Yes?

ZIP. Where is our point-five child?

SOOS. Hidden in the attic. *(They laugh.)*

ZIP. And we're so proud of her. *(Their laughter becomes wild.)*

SOOS. She's half a person, but we're fully proud. We are so proud.

ZIP. We are too sick. *(They catch their breath. The game is over. The laughing stops.)*

SOOS. Oh, God. Do we have nothing to be proud of? There must be something.

ZIP. *(Silence. Seriously.)* I'm proud to be an American. *(A second. They look at each other. They burst into laughter.)*

SOOS. Oh, God, could we get a little more jaded?

ZIP. We are just the worst.

SOOS. Two peas in the proverbial pod.

ZIP. You're the only one I can laugh with.

SOOS. Same here.

ZIP. I love you.

SOOS. I love you, too.

ZIP. God.

SOOS. I love you.

ZIP. I love you. *(She kisses him. A moment. She leans in to kiss him again. He stops her.)* We're friends.

SOOS. That can be enough.

ZIP. Please don't.

SOOS. It could be a start.

ZIP. Soos. C'mon. No.

SOOS. I don't know.

ZIP. No. I don't know, either.

SOOS. Do you want to get married?

ZIP. To each other?

SOOS. Yeah. Sure.

ZIP. And have like the Boulevard house?

SOOS. I don't know. Yeah.

ZIP. We just made fun of all that.

SOOS. I make fun of things sometimes because I want them.

ZIP. I don't know, marriage? I mean ... our kids would look great.

SOOS. Oh, the bone structure? Forget it.

ZIP. But marriage is such a ... I just don't think so. Does that hurt your feelings?

SOOS. Whatever.

ZIP. Are you like depressed and empty? I mean, more than usual?

SOOS. Yeah. Sure.

ZIP. Yeah?

SOOS. Yeah. A lot, anymore.

ZIP. Me too. I think about Chloe and the — whatever we had and I feel kind of —

SOOS. Depressed and empty?

ZIP. Yeah.

SOOS. I feel that.

ZIP. Yeah?

SOOS. When I think of Walker. My ex-husband.

ZIP. Right.

SOOS. It's bad.

ZIP. Hmmmm.

SOOS. Terrible bad.

ZIP. Yes.

SOOS. But maybe there's comfort in that ... you only have to go through that kind of love, you know, once.

ZIP. Well. *(Pause.)* Well. Maybe we should be looking for those kinds of love again. Maybe.

SOOS. Zip, I hate to tell you, but I'm sick of being young. I'm sick of waiting to be an adult. I want to get the fuck out of the cub room. And I ... just want to start having a life with something vaguely resembling dignity.

ZIP. Oh Soos.

SOOS. You see, I don't want anything special anymore, Zip. I don't want Paris. I don't want the emeralds and Parker Stevenson. I just want to get through my life unlonely and to believe. To believe in something. With maybe some laughs along the way. It's not much, but already it's turning out to be a real tall order. A real unheard-of request.

ZIP. C'mon, now. You —

SOOS. I know. I know. I know I know I know. I know I'm not, you know, impoverished and foraging through rubbish for tossed sandwiches. I know I'm not stretched out in a hospital bed valiantly fighting off some disease. I know I have everything going for me. But I still feel … nothing. So if I have everything going for me and I feel … nothing. What does that say about everything? *(Pause.)*

ZIP.   Are you scared?

SOOS.   Yes.

ZIP.   Are you lonely?

SOOS.   Yes.

ZIP.   Marry me.

SOOS.   Why?

ZIP.   Because I'm scared and lonely, too. And.

SOOS.   And?

ZIP.   And. Hell. We'll have some laughs. *(They stare at one another, neither knowing what to do. Then with quiet humility, Zip gets down on one knee.)*

SOOS.   Oh God. Yes. Yes. I will marry you, Mr. Thomas Benum Mueller the Third. I will become Mrs. the Third. *(They laugh and hold one another.)* Zip?

ZIP.   Still here.

SOOS.   I'm still scared. *(They don't kiss. They hold one another. For dear life.)*

END OF PLAY

PROPERTY LIST

Cigarettes
Matches or lighter
Beer/cooler of beer
Coffee mugs
Old wooden lighter (POOKER)
Pillow (SOOS)
Magazine (BRI, ZIP)
Drink (SOOS)
Purse (ZIP)
Wastepaper basket (ZIP)
Citronella candle (CHLOE)
Blanket (CHLOE, ZIP)
Underwear (ZIP)
Bottle of Asti (SOOS)
Tall glass (SOOS)